Ukulele *from the* Beginning

Published by
Chester Music Limited

Exclusive Distributors:
Hal Leonard
7777 West Bluemound Road
Milwaukee, WI 53213
Email: info@halleonard.com

Hal Leonard Europe Limited
42 Wigmore Street
Marylebone, London, W1U 2RY
Email: info@halleonardeurope.com

Hal Leonard Australia Pty. Ltd.
4 Lentara Court
Cheltenham, Victoria, 3192 Australia
Email: info@halleonard.com.au

This book © Copyright 2007 Chester Music.
All rights reserved. International copyright secured.

For all works contained herein:
Unauthorized copying, arranging, adapting, recording, Internet posting, public performance, or other distribution of the music in this publication is an infringement of copyright.
Infringers are liable under the law.

Written by Tim Fulston
Illustrations by Benedict Siddle
Processing and layout by Camden Music, London.
Edited by Rachel Payne

Printed in the EU.

www.halleonard.com

About the book

This book is the ideal introduction to one of today's most popular little instruments. Versatile and adaptable, the ukulele has been around since the late nineteenth century and is now enjoying a remarkable surge of popularity. It's inexpensive, easy to learn and suitable for playing all kinds of music.

Ukulele from the Beginning helps you make the most of the uke's many virtues. Even beginners soon find they can make music using simple, easy-to-play chords on an instrument that even small hands can master!

No musical knowledge is necessary to get started and before long almost anyone can play accompaniments to simple tunes. All of which makes the ukulele the ideal classroom instrument. Any teacher, with or without musical knowledge, will discover that by using *Ukulele from the Beginning* it's simple to teach basic chords by playing along with-known favourite songs. The ukulele is a great place to start enjoying music in the classroom and this book makes the process a pleasure for teacher and children alike.

Contents

Page	Tune Title	New Chords / Musical Points
4	Getting Started	
	Strings and Tuning	
5	Chords	C, G7
6	Reading Music	
	Notes and Values	
7	Animal Fair	Repeat sign
8	London Bridge	
9	A New Chord	F
10	This Old Man	
11	Old Macdonald	
12	Waltzing Matilda	
14	John Brown's Body	
15	Oh When The Saints	
16	Oh! Susanna	
18	Camptown Races	
20	Ten Green Bottles	

Page	Tune Title	New Chords / Musical Points
21	If You're Happy	
22	More Seventh Chords	C7, D7
23	Row, Row, Row Your Boat	Swing Rhythms
24	She'll Be Coming Round The Mountain	
25	Jingle Bells	Ostinato
26	Minor Chords	Am, Dm
	Up-strokes	
27	Drunken Sailor	
28	My Grandfather's Clock	
30	Where Did You Get That Hat?	
32	Loch Lomond	Dotted Rhythms
33	More Chords	Gm, E7
34	Cockles and Mussels	
36	Mulberry Bush	
37	Greensleeves	
38	I'm Henery The Eighth, I Am	

Getting started

Welcome to Ukulele From The Beginning. If you're new to the instrument, you'll need to know a few basic things before you can start playing.

Strings & Tuning

The ukulele's four strings are tuned to the following notes:

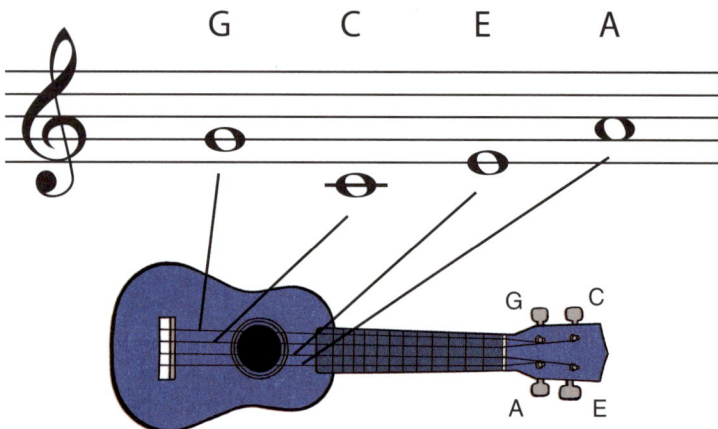

You can find these notes on a piano or use an electronic tuner. Turn each tuning peg until the string reaches the same pitch as the tuning note—turning clockwise makes the note higher, anti-clockwise makes it lower.

Chords

Rather than playing single notes as you might on a recorder or violin, most ukulele playing involves strumming all four strings at once. The sound you make will depend on where you place your left-hand fingers. The word for several notes played together is 'chord'—all the music in this book contains chord symbols so you know which chords to play. These usually have simple names like C and F; some have longer names like G7 ("G seven") and Am ("A minor").

The easiest way to learn a new chord is a **chord box**. This shows the strings as vertical lines, the frets as horizontal lines and the fingers as numbered dots or circles. The circle means that you play an open string.

The first song in this book uses just one chord! Here it is.

This box means: place your 3rd left hand finger at the 3rd fret on the A string.

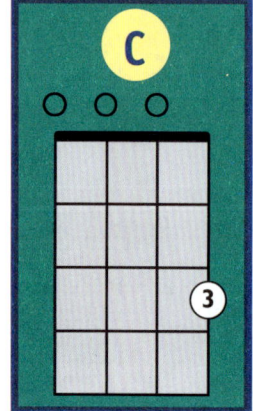

So when you see the 'C' chord symbol in any song in this book, all you need is your third finger. Just make sure you get it in the right place!

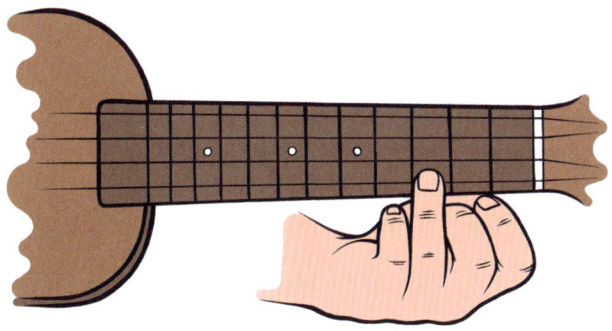

Strum all four strings with your right hand, using either your thumb or all your fingers together. For our first few songs, simply strum downwards on each beat:

For the next few songs, you'll need one more chord:

Practise getting your fingers round these before starting the songs!

Reading Music

It's best to learn the ukulele as an accompaniment to singing, so this books is full of songs we hope you know so you can sing and play. To play the ukulele you don't need to read music, but we have written out the tunes in this book under the chord symbols to help you know when to play (or they could be played on another instrument).

The tune has been written on the **stave**. This is made of five lines. The position of the note on the stave tells you how high or low it is.

Time signature   Bar

Music is written in bars, to help organise the rhythm. The **time signature** tells you how many beats are in a bar (the top number) and what type of beat (underneath).

Notes and values

𝅝 Semibreve or Whole Note
Equals four crotchets—play the note for four counts.

𝅗𝅥 Minim or Half Note
Equals two crotchets—play the note for two counts.

♩ Crotchet or Quarter Note
One crotchet equals one count.

♪ Quaver or Eighth Note
Equals half a crotchet—play the note for half a count.

𝅘𝅥𝅯 Semi-quaver or Sixteenth Note
Equals a quarter of a crotchet—play the note for a quarter of a count.

The example above therefore has four crotchets in every bar. Different time signatures create different feels.

Animal Fair

Say the words out loud and in rhythm. Clap a steady beat as you do this. You should find that you are clapping twice in every bar—on the first and fourth quavers. This is how the beat is grouped when there are six quavers in every bar (in threes). Strum on these beats.

Repeat signs

These tell you to play all the music between the signs twice. The first time through you play the bar with the number 1 above and the second time you jump to the bar with the number 2 above and carry on!

London Bridge

Say the words out loud and in rhythm. Clap a steady beat as you do this.

You should find that you are clapping four times in every bar (on every crotchet). This is how the beat is grouped when there are four crotchets in a bar. Strum on these beats.

> **Repeat signs**
>
> When the music should be repeated from the very beginning you do not need the first repeat sign—just the second.

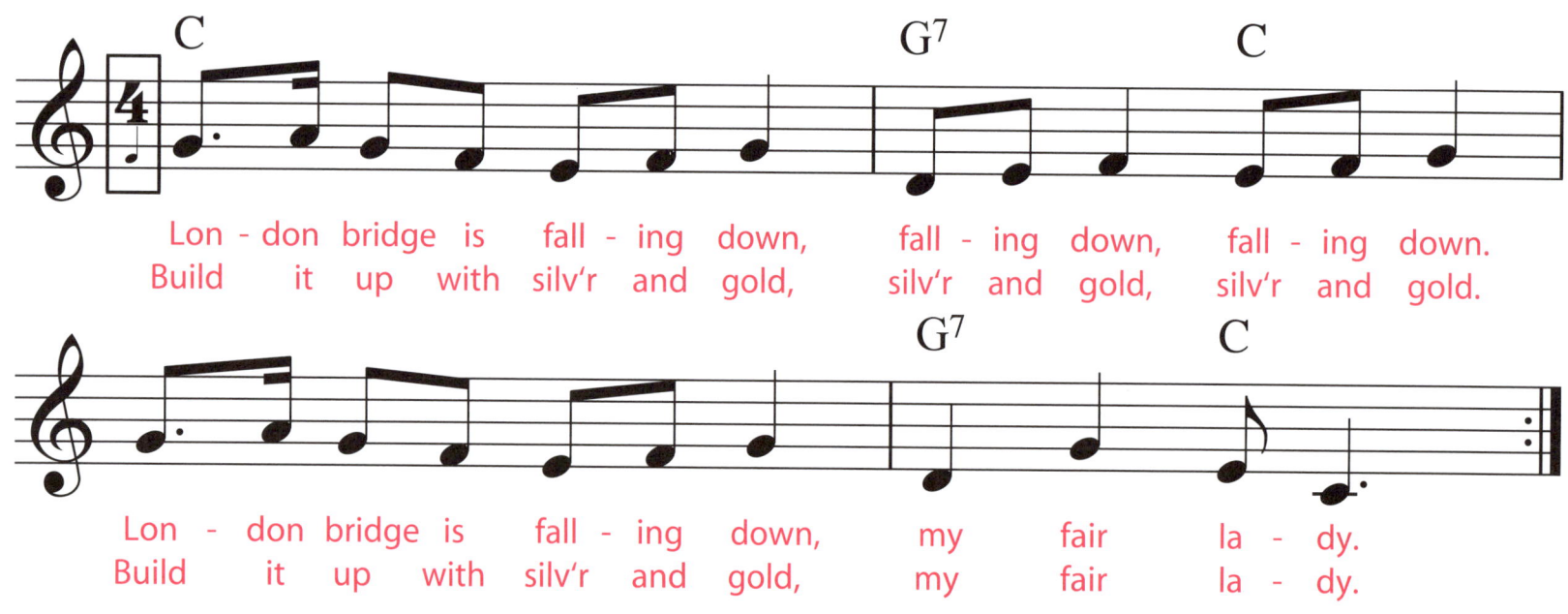

A New Chord

The F chord uses two fingers:

Tips!

Any fingers that are not used should still hover just above the fretboard—don't tuck them away behind the neck!

Don't move your fingers more than you have to. Changing from F to G7 is easy as the first finger stays put and the second finger only has to move across from the G string to the C string.

This Old Man

Say the words to this song out loud and in rhythm. Clap a steady beat as you do this.

You should find that you are clapping two times in every bar (on each crotchet). This is where the beat falls when we have two crotchets in a bar. Strum on these beats.

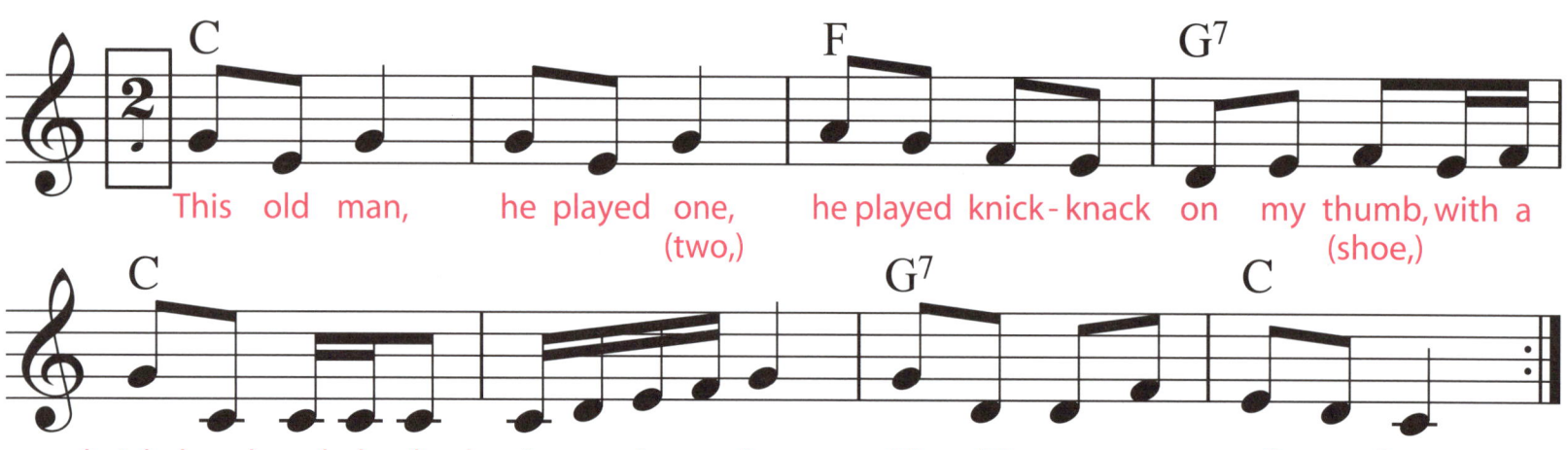

four... door
five... hive
six... sticks
seven... up in heaven

eight... gate
nine... line
ten... once again

Old Macdonald

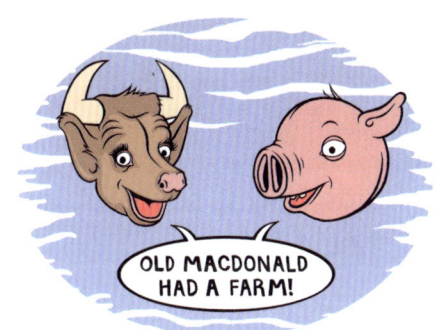

OLD MACDONALD
HAD A FARM!

Say the words to this song out loud and in rhythm. Clap a steady beat as you do this. Strum on these beats. Keep thinking ahead to the next chord so you are ready in time.

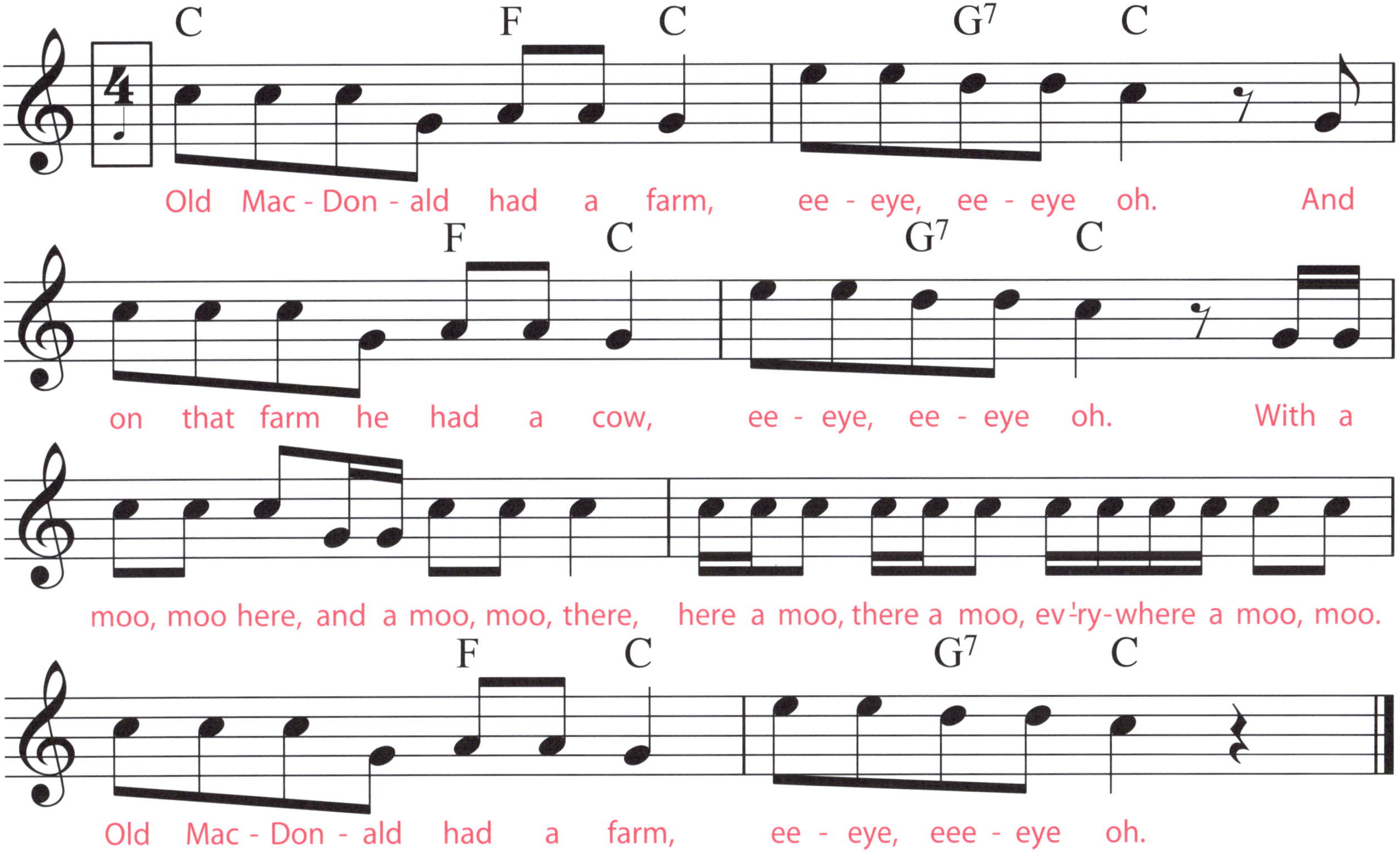
C F C G7 C
Old Mac - Don - ald had a farm, ee - eye, ee - eye oh. And
F C G7 C
on that farm he had a cow, ee - eye, ee - eye oh. With a
moo, moo here, and a moo, moo, there, here a moo, there a moo, ev'-ry-where a moo, moo.
F C G7 C
Old Mac - Don - ald had a farm, ee - eye, eee - eye oh.

Waltzing Matilda

Say the words to this song out loud and in rhythm. Clap a steady beat as you do this. It is on these beats that you should strum.

Keep thinking ahead for your chord changes.

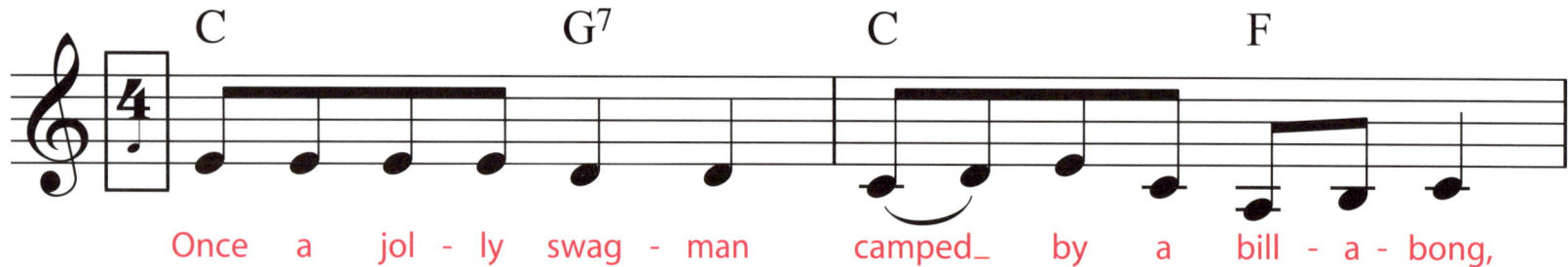

Once a jol - ly swag - man camped by a bill - a - bong,

un - der the shade of a cool - a - bah tree. And he sang as he watched and

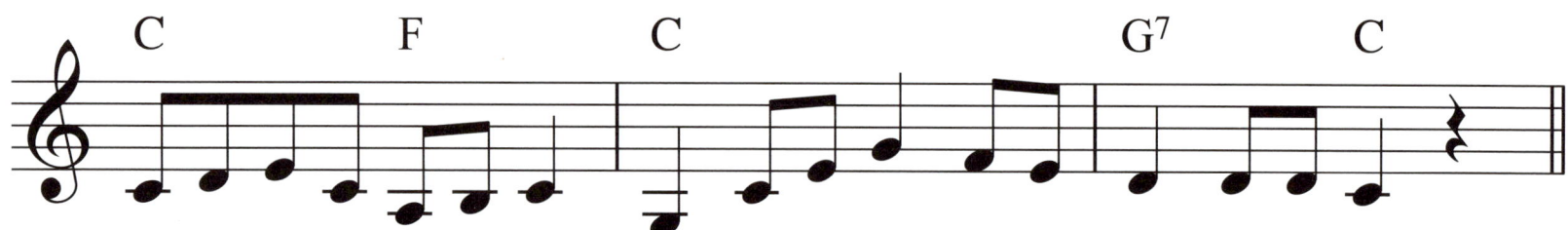

wait - ed 'til his bil - ly boiled: "Who'll come a waltz - ing Ma - til - da with me?

John Brown's Body

Say the words out loud and in rhythm. Clap a steady beat as you do this (every crotchet—look at the time signature!). Sing the song, and strum on these beats.
When you say or sing the tune you might notice that the quavers in the tune are not given equal lengths—they are a long followed by a short. We call this a **swung rhythm**.

Oh When The Saints

Say the words to this song out loud and in rhythm. Clap a steady beat as you do this. Strum on these beats (every minim!).

This piece is like a march. Keep it steady and strong, imagine you are walking to the beat.

Idea: Get a drum to march along with you on the first beat of every bar.

Oh! Susanna

Look at the time signature (you're getting used to this now!)—two minims in every bar, so we strum twice in every bar, on the minim beat.

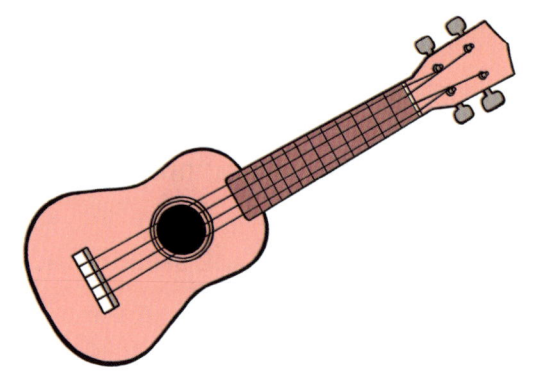

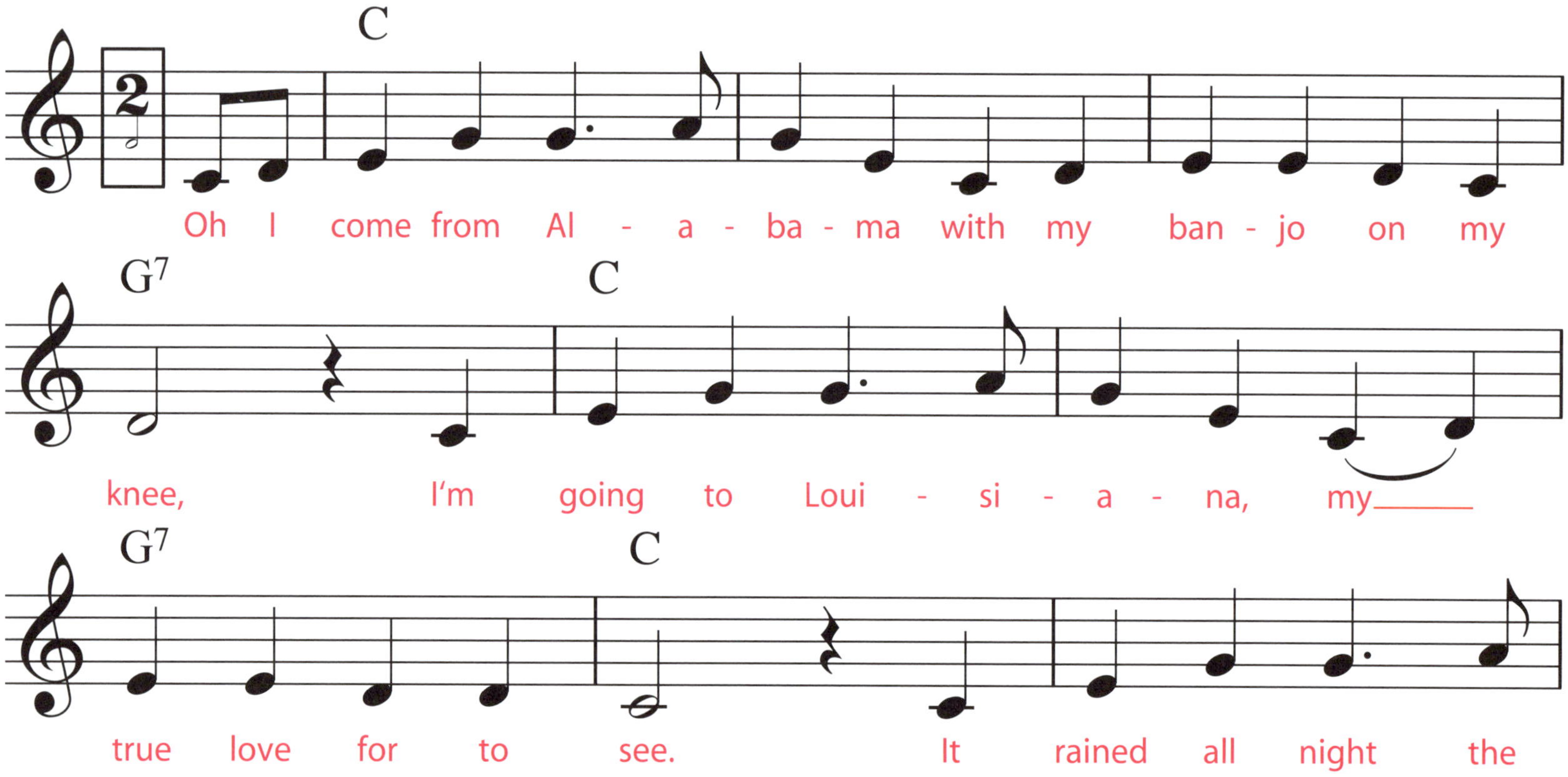
C
Oh I come from Al - a - ba - ma with my ban - jo on my
G7
C
knee, I'm going to Loui - si - a - na, my
G7
C
true love for to see. It rained all night the

Camptown Races

Say the words out loud and in rhythm, and clap the steady beat. Strum on these beats.

Remember to carry on and play the second page once you have repeated the first.

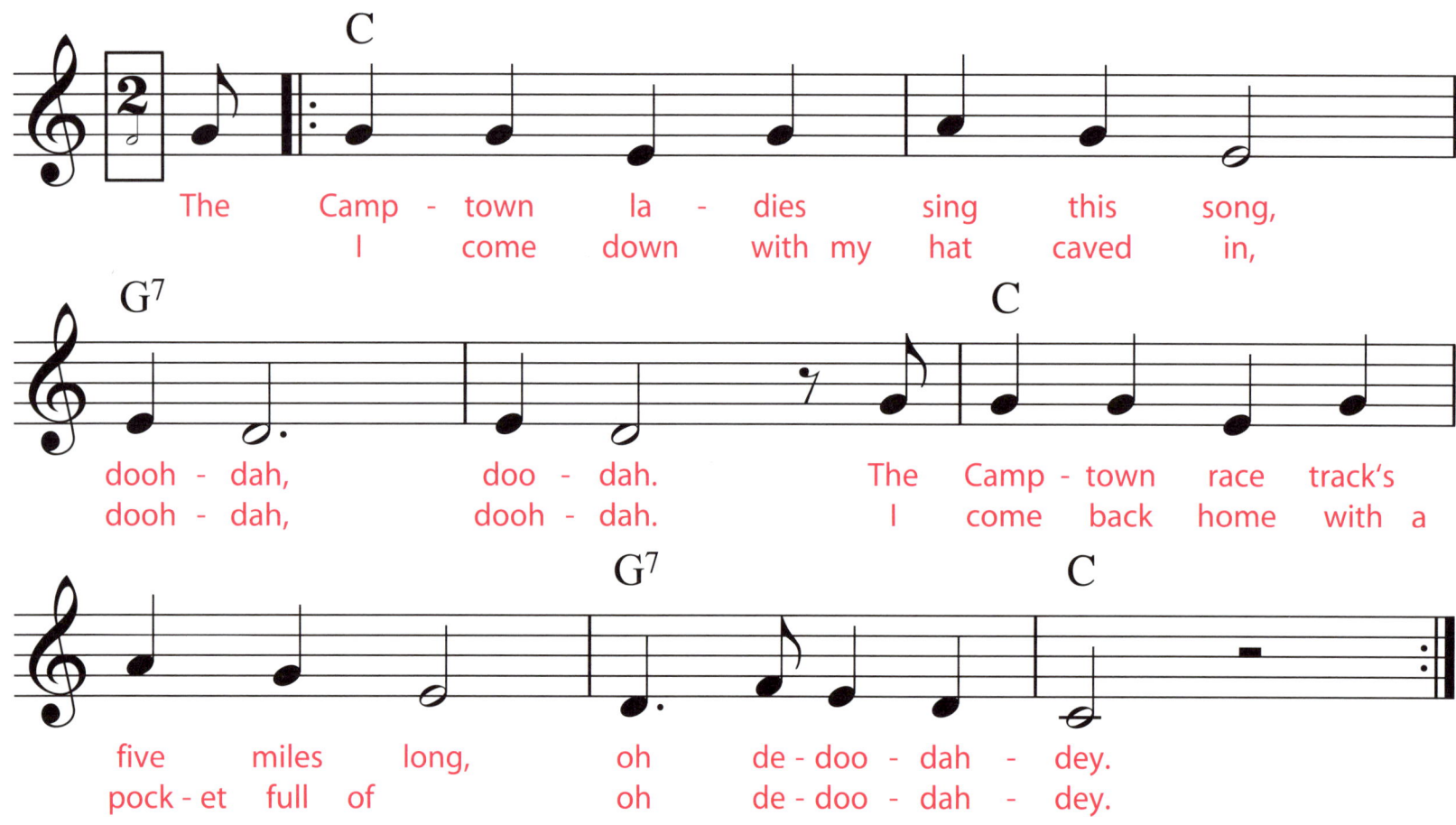

Ten Green Bottles

Say the words to this song out loud and in rhythm whilst you clap the beat. Strum on these beats.

You might notice it is swung, listen when you sing 'hanging on the wall'—it skips along. It is easy to rush songs that are swung, so keep your strumming steady, and don't let your singing run away!

Ten green bot-tles hang-ing on the wall,
Nine... etc.
ten green bot-tles hang-ing on the wall. But if one green bot-tle should ac-ci-dent-'ly fall, there'll be nine green bot-tles hang-ing on the wall.

If You're Happy

Say the words out loud and in rhythm whilst clapping the beat. Strum on these beats.

Idea: You could tap your ukulele body (softly) when it tells you to clap!

If you're hap-py and you know it clap your hands, if you're

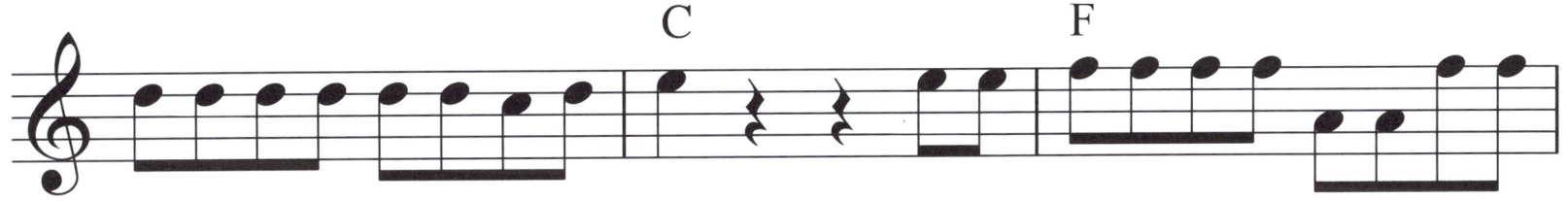

hap-py and you know it clap your hands. If you're hap-py and you know it and you

real-ly want to show it, if you're hap-py and you know it clap your hands.

More Seventh Chords

You'll need two new seventh chords for the next few songs.

 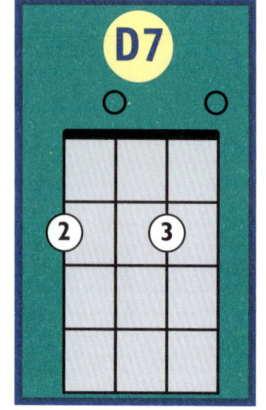 

Tips!

The C7 chord is another really easy chord. One way of changing from C to C7 very smoothly is to have the first finger ready at the first fret *behind* the third finger, while playing the C chord.

Seventh chords have a richer sound than simple chords like C and F.

Row, Row, Row Your Boat

Say the words out loud and in rhythm whilst clapping the beat. (We have four crotchets in every bar so this should be every crotchet beat.)

More about swung rhythms
When music is swung, each beat is split into three, not two. A pair of quavers becomes a *long* quaver (the first two-thirds of the beat) followed by a *short* one (the final third). It also means you can fit three equal notes into one crotchet beat (sing 'mer-ri-ly, mer-ri-ly' to get the idea). We show that this is happening by writing a '3' above the notes. These three together are known as **triplets**.

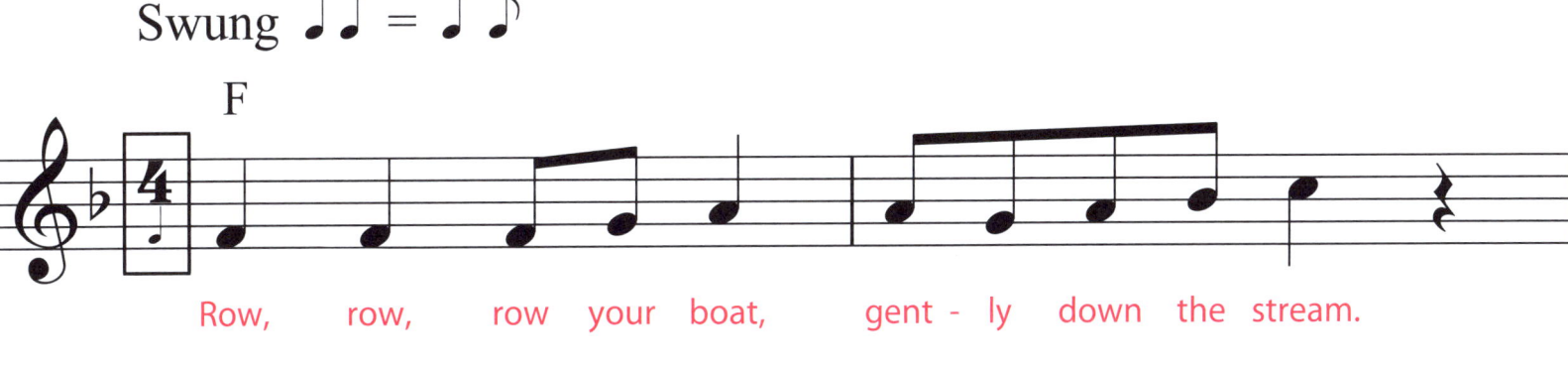

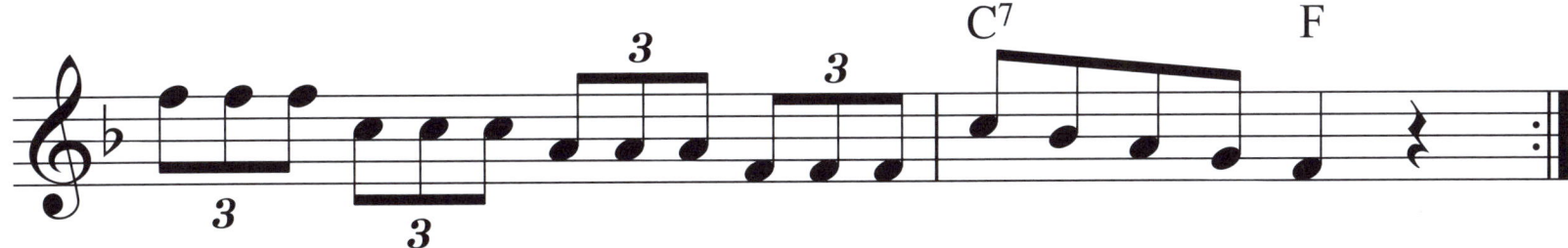

She'll Be Coming Round The Mountain

Say the words out loud and in rhythm whilst clapping the beat*. Strum on these beats.

*See p15 if you can't remember where the beat should fall for this time signature.

Jingle Bells

Say the words out loud and in rhythm whilst clapping the beat. Strum on these beats.

Idea: Can you get someone to tap the steady beat on some sleighbells?

Jin-gle bells, jin-gle bells, jin-gle all the way. Oh what fun it is to ride in a

one horse op-en sleigh. Oh, jin-gle bells, jin-gle bells, jin-gle all the way.

Oh what fun it is to ride in a one-horse op-en sleigh.

Minor Chords

These chords have a different sound which is sometimes described as sad.

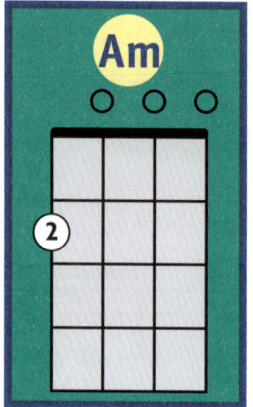 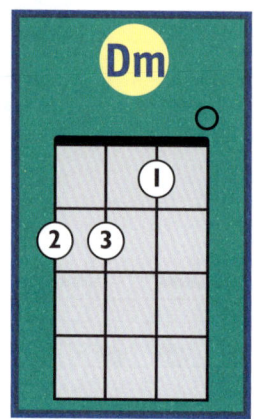

Tips!

The Am chord is easy—just remove the first finger from the F chord shape.

Up-Strokes

Playing just down-strokes on the beat can get a little boring. Try adding up-strokes between the beats:

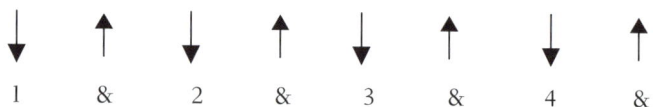

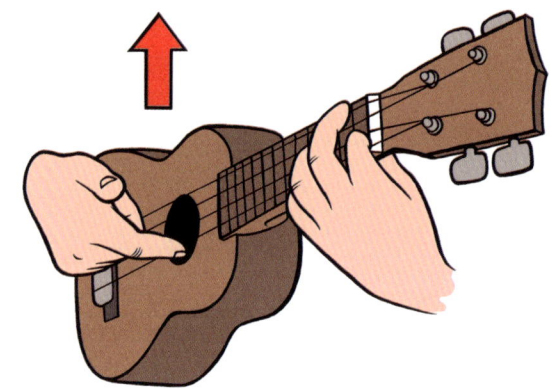

Drunken Sailor

Say the words out loud and in rhythm whilst clapping the beat.
Strum down-strokes on these beats, and put upstrokes between them.

This piece is in the key of D minor, meaning that D minor is its 'home chord'. Can you hear how it sounds different?

Idea:
Split the class in two. One group plays the Dm bars, and the other plays the C chords. The group who is not strumming should do the singing!

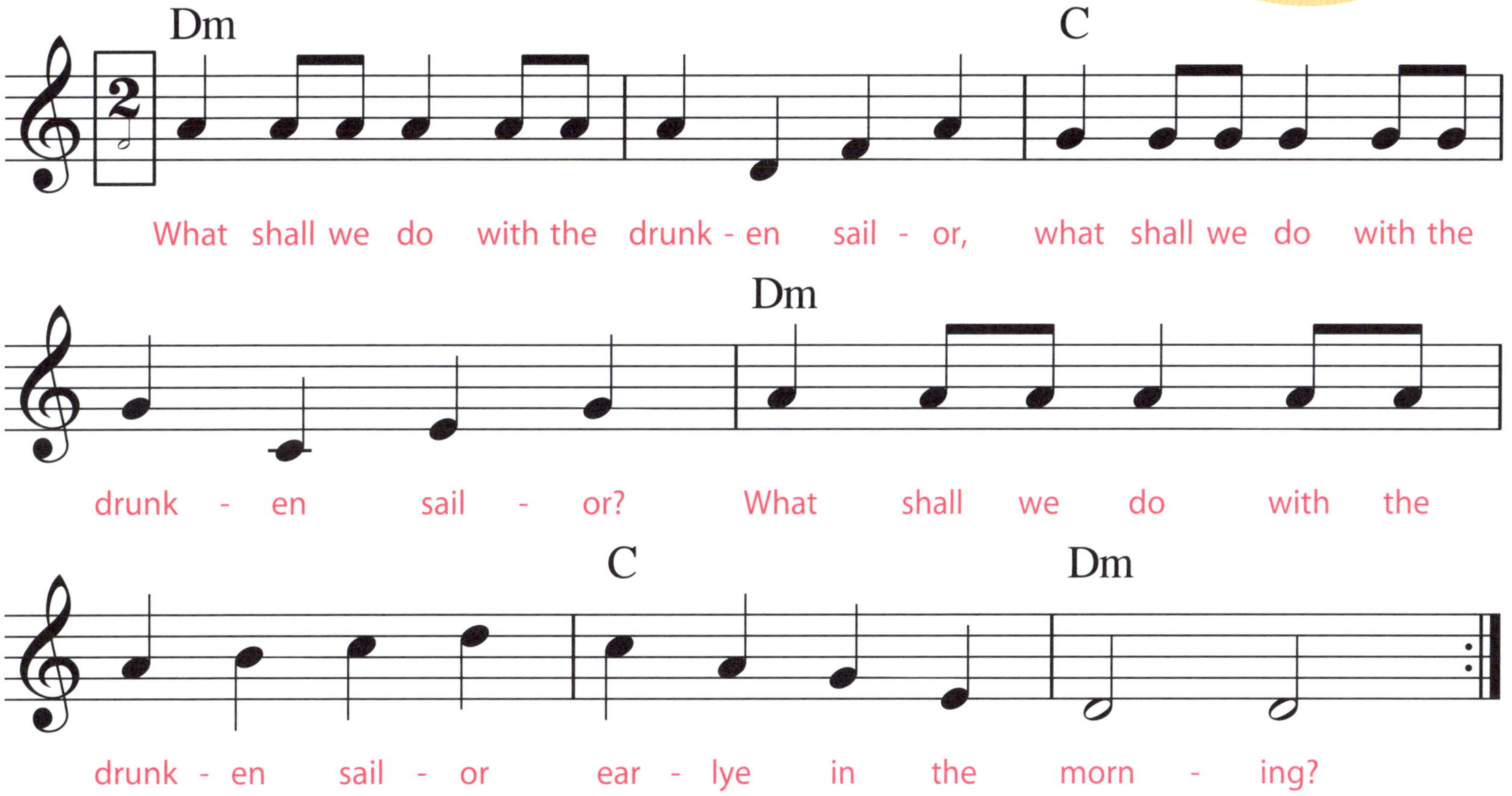

What shall we do with the drunk - en sail - or, what shall we do with the drunk - en sail - or? What shall we do with the drunk - en sail - or ear - lye in the morn - ing?

My Grandfather's Clock

This song not only has lots of chord changes, but we are adding up-strokes too. It's a bit of a musical tongue-twister! Take your time, practise slowly first and always think ahead!

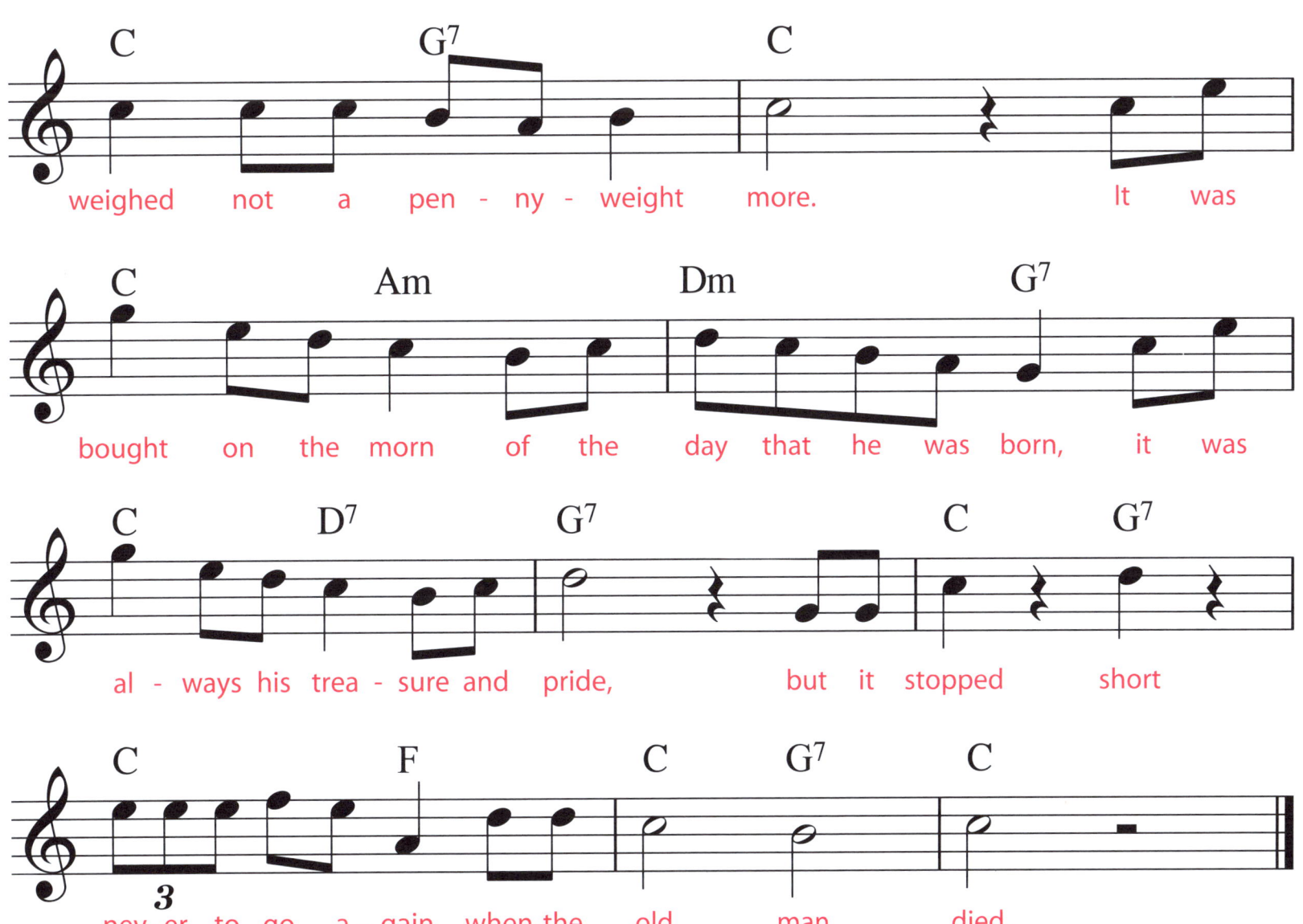

Where Did You Get That Hat?

Say the words out loud and in rhythm whilst clapping the beat. There are a number of faster chord changes in this piece so keep steady and keep thinking ahead.

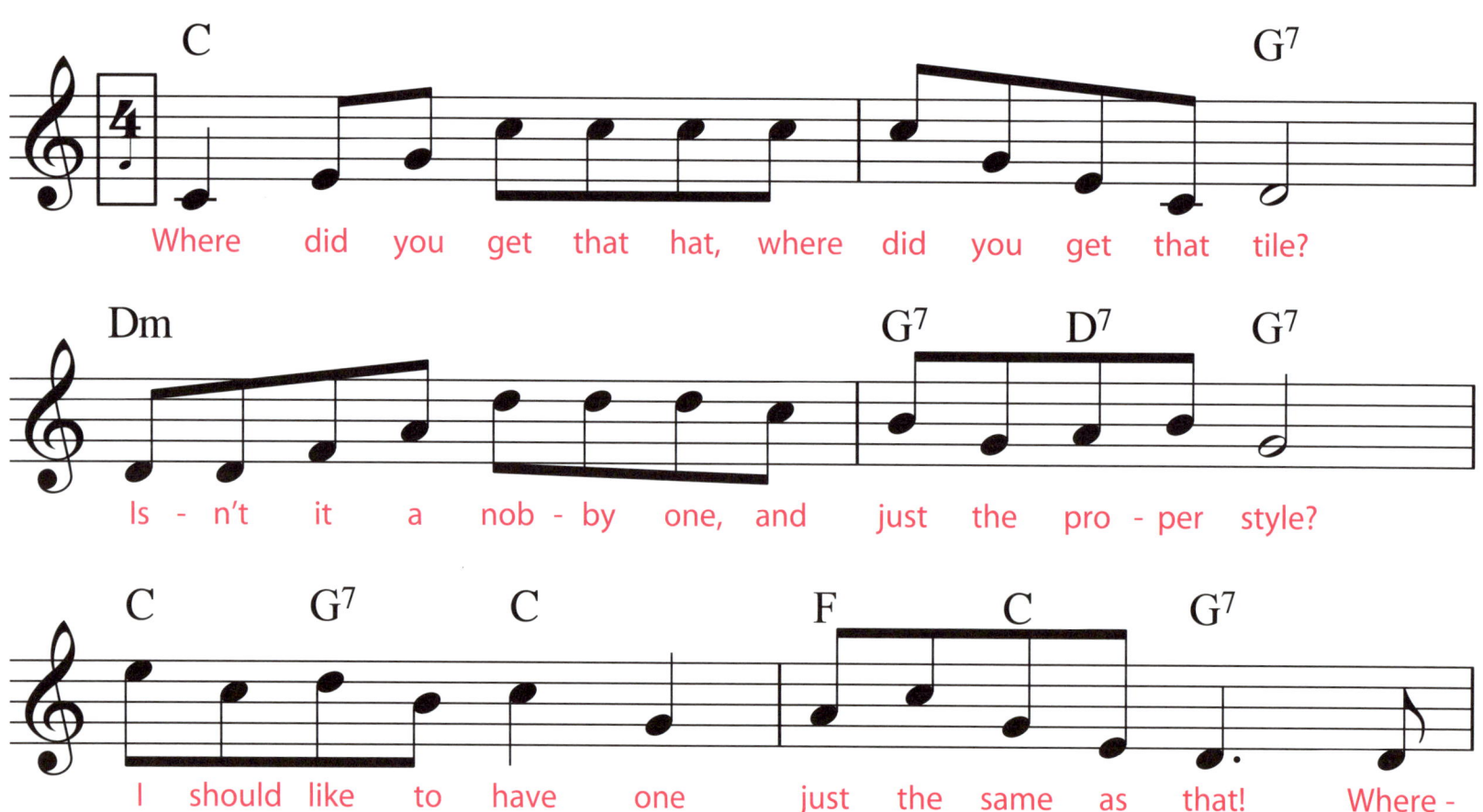

Loch Lomond

Dotted rhythms

You might have noticed this rhythm in the tune:

Listen to yourself say or sing the words and you should hear a long note followed by a short. The dot means increase the note length by half. So the dotted quaver lasts for ¾ beat, and the semiquaver lasts for ¼ beat (as normal). Listen again to how it sounds.

Idea: This tune would sound perfect on a keyboard pipe sound. Do you have some people who could play the tune while you strum?

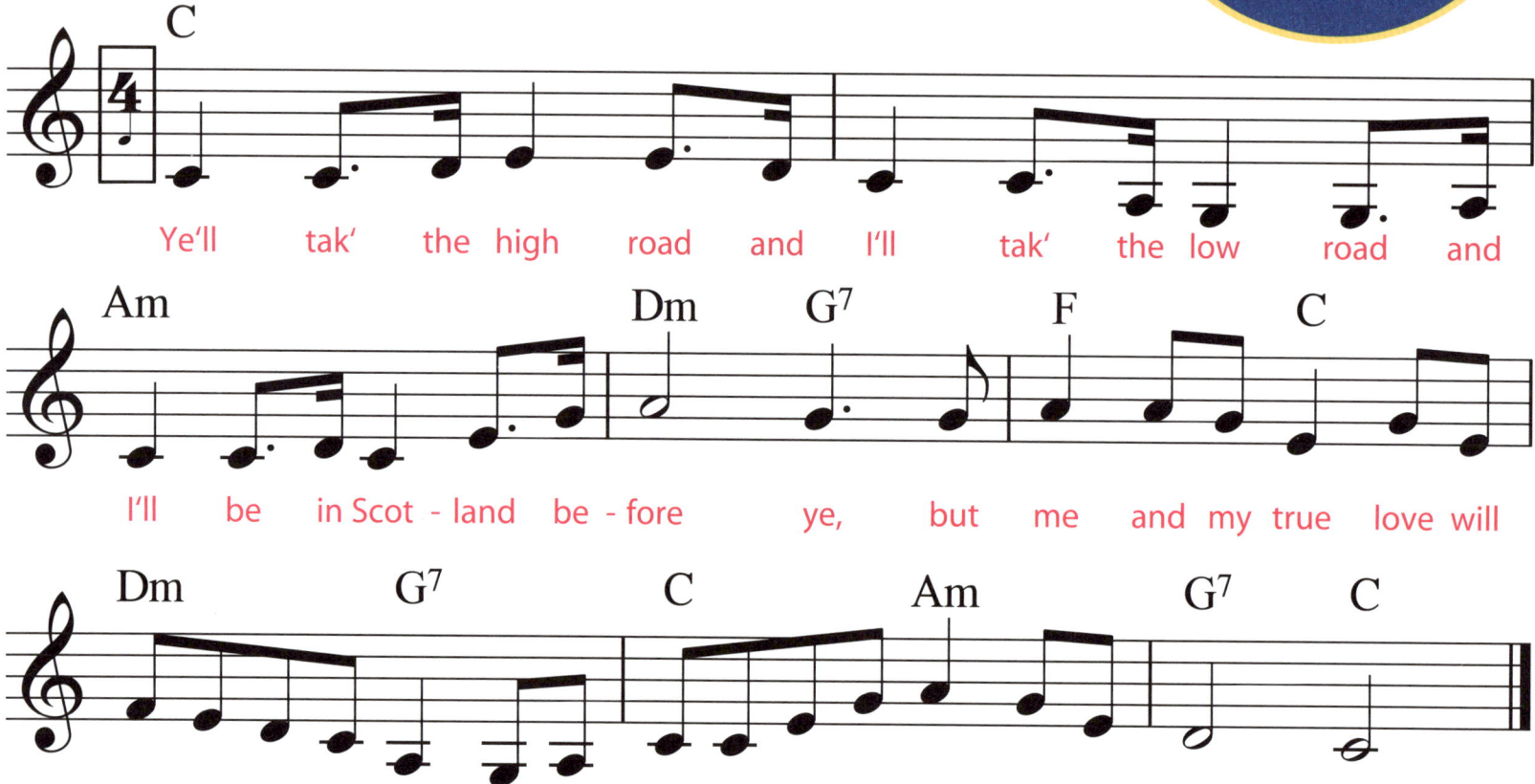

Ye'll tak' the high road and I'll tak' the low road and I'll be in Scot-land be-fore ye, but me and my true love will nev-er meet a-gain on the bon-nie, bon-nie banks of Loch Lo - mond.

More Chords

You'll need a couple more chords for the last few songs.

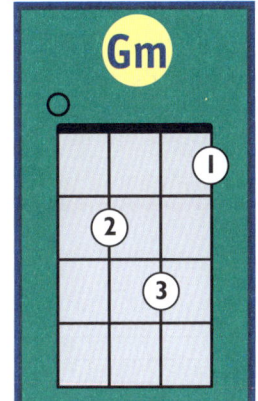
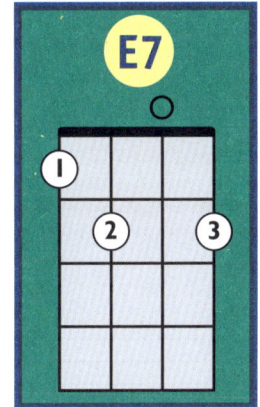

If you've learned all the shapes in this book, you now know nine chords! You can use these to play many other songs too. See if you can work out the chord changes to some of the following songs:

How Much Is That Doggie In The Window? (using C and G7)
Bobby Shafto (using C, F and G7)
Oh Dear, What Can The Matter Be? (C, G7, Dm and Am)

Cockles and Mussels

Say the words to this song out loud and in rhythm whilst clapping the steady beat. This piece has three crotchet beats in every bar so we will play our down-strokes on these beats. Can you decide which beats to put up-strokes between? Maybe you could do different things in the chorus to the verse and mark arrows on the music so you don't forget and so you all do the same thing!

Dotted rhythms

We have these in this song back to front and the right way round! Can you spot them? Listen to their different sounds.

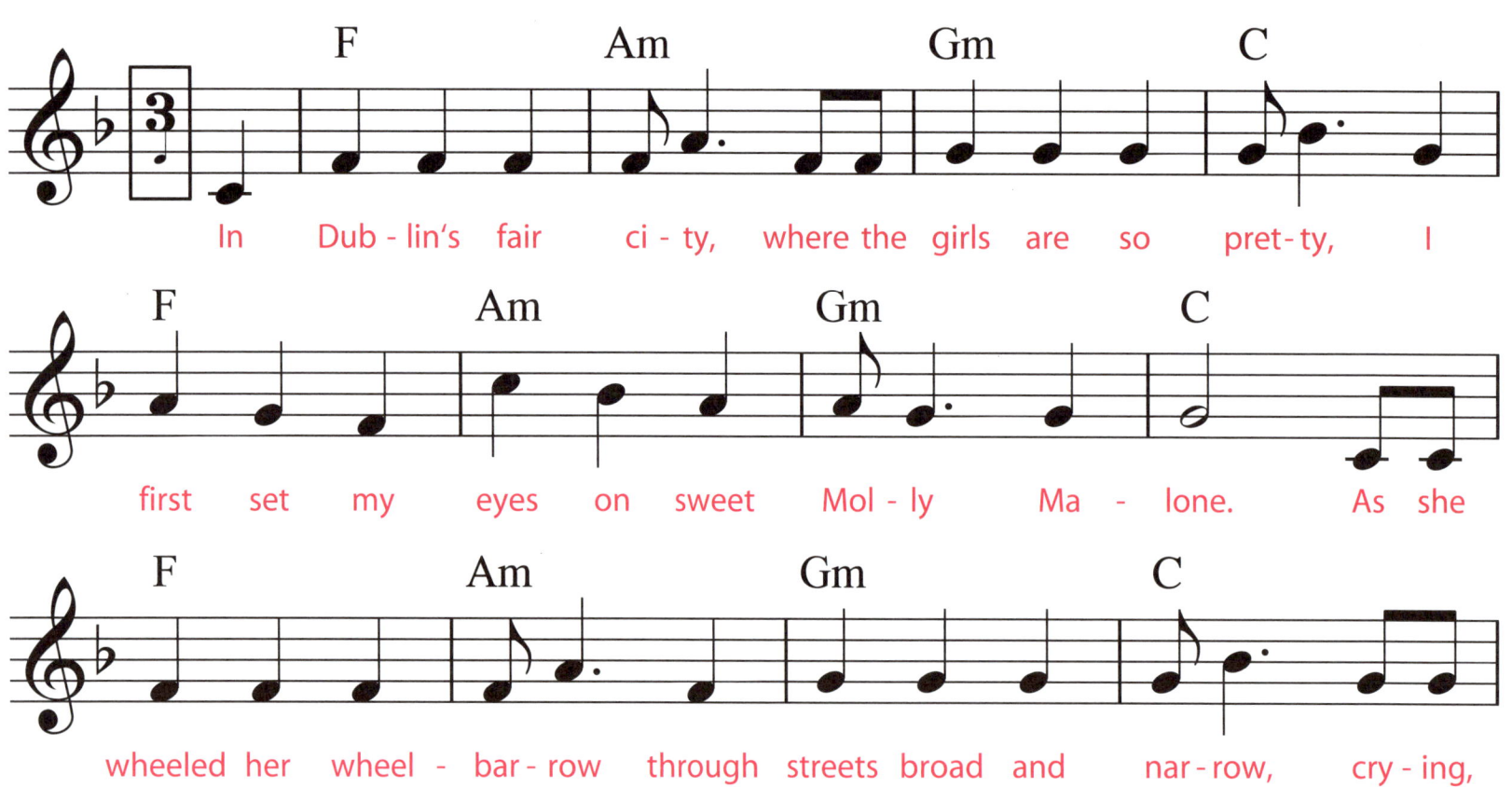

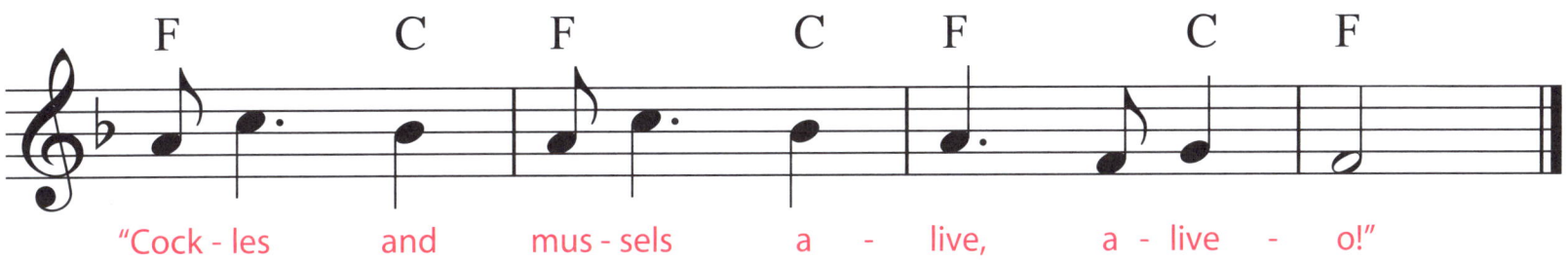

Mulberry Bush

Look at the time signature, we have seen this before but a long time ago! Because this time signature groups the music in threes try a downstroke on the first and fourth quavers, and an upstroke on the third and sixth. This gives a longer strum on the down than the up. Write the arrows on your music in pencil if that helps!

Here we go round the mul - b'ry bush, the mul - b'ry bush, the mul - b'ry bush.

Here we go round the mul - b'ry bush on a cold and frost - y mor - ning.

Greensleeves

This piece has the same time signature again, so try the same strumming pattern.
It also has dotted rhythms in the melody—can you hear them? They create a skip to the next note!

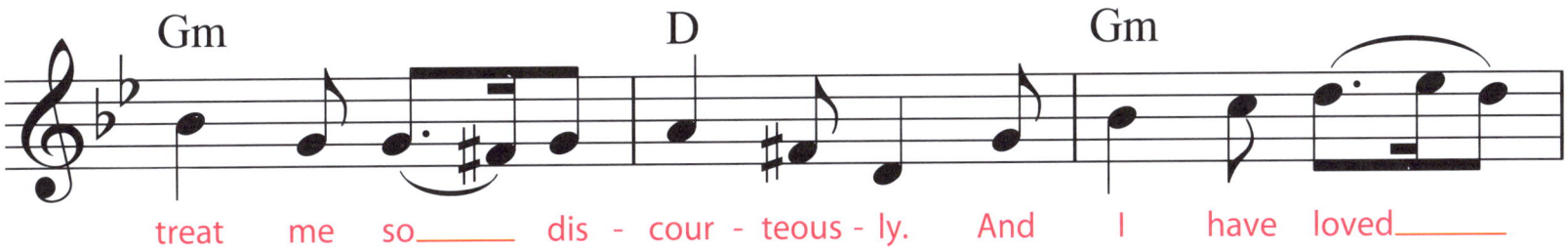

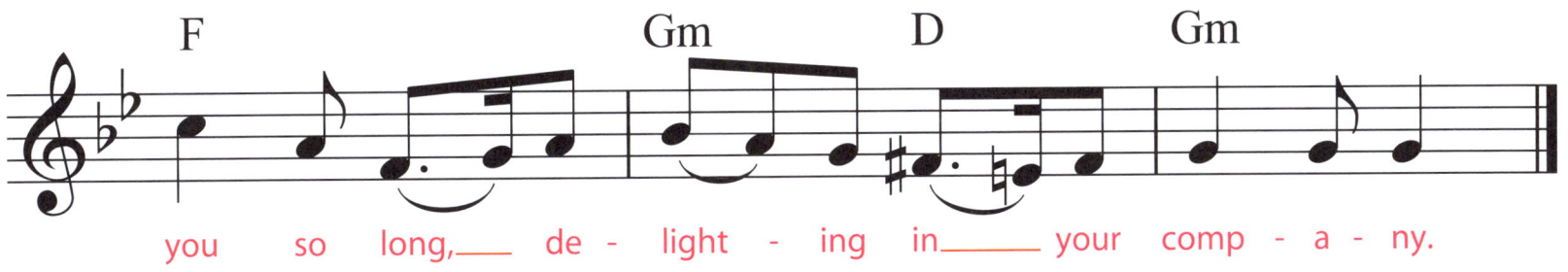

I'm Henery The Eighth, I Am

We're at our last piece now. Well done!
For this one you can decide your own strumming pattern—
try to add variety and colour by changing how you strum!

I'm Hen - e - ry the Eighth, I am.
Hen - e - ry the Eighth I am, I am. I got mar-ried to the
wid - ow next door; she's been mar - ried sev - en

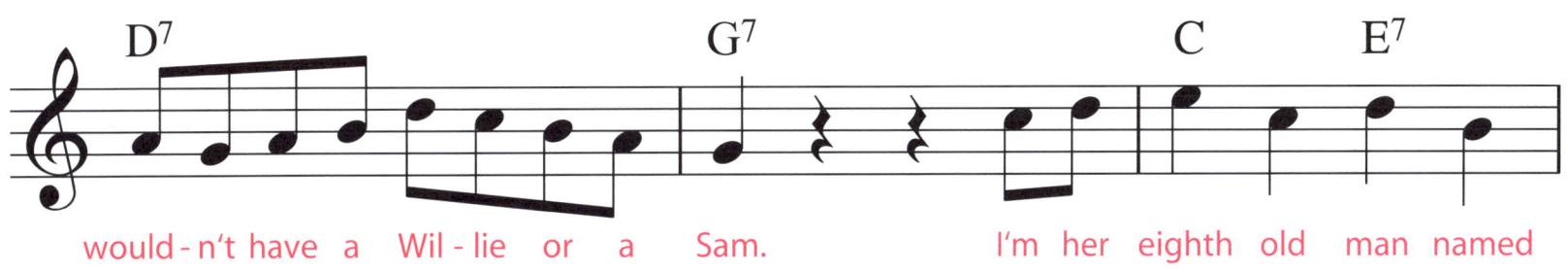